Books by Mark Strand

POETRY

Blizzard of One   1998
Dark Harbor   1993
Reasons for Moving, Darker, & the Sargentville Notebook   1992
The Continuous Life   1990
Selected Poems   1980
The Late Hour   1978
The Story of Our Lives   1973
Darker   1970
Reasons for Moving   1968
Sleeping with One Eye Open   1964

PROSE

The Weather of Words   2000
Mr. and Mrs. Baby   1985
The Monument   1978

TRANSLATIONS

Travelling in the Family   1986
(POEMS BY CARLOS DRUMMOND DE ANDRADE,
WITH THOMAS COLCHIE)

The Owl's Insomnia   1973
(POEMS BY RAFAEL ALBERTI)

ART BOOKS

Edward Hopper   1993
William Bailey   1987
Art of the Real   1983

FOR CHILDREN

Rembrandt Takes a Walk   1986
The Night Book   1985
The Planet of Lost Things   1972

ANTHOLOGIES

The Golden Ecco Anthology   1994
The Best American Poetry (WITH DAVID LEHMAN)   1991
Another Republic (WITH CHARLES SIMIC)   1975
New Poetry of Mexico (WITH OCTAVIO PAZ)   1970
The Contemporary American Poets   1969

Dark Harbor

Mark Strand

DARK HARBOR

A POEM

Alfred A. Knopf   New York   2012

THIS IS A BORZOI BOOK
PUBLISHED BY ALFRED A. KNOPF, INC.

www.randomhouse.com/knopf/poetry/

ACKNOWLEDGMENTS
Selections from this poem have appeared in the following magazines:

Antaeus VIII, XXX, XXXVI, XXXVIII, XLI
New Republic XX, XXXII, XLIV
New Yorker I, III, IV, XI, XIII, XIV, XV, XVI, XXI, XXXI, XXXV, XL
Paris Review II, V, XVII, XVIII, XIX
Partisan Review VII, IX, XLIII
Seems XII, XXIV, XXXIV
Weber Studies XXXIX, XLII, XLV
Yale Review VI, X, XXV

The author is grateful to the John D. and Catherine T. MacArthur Foundation for a fellowship that was of great help in writing this book.

Library of Congress Cataloging-in-Publication Data

Strand, Mark
    Dark harbor : a poem / by Mark Strand. — 1st ed.
        p.   cm.
    ISBN 0-679-75279-X
    I. Title.
PS3569.T69D28   1993   92-19983
811'.54—dc20   CIP

    ISBN 978-0-679-75279-0

Hardcover Edition Published March 22, 1993
Paperback Edition Published July 3, 1994

146028962

TO BILL AND SANDY BAILEY

PROEM

"This is my Main Street," he said as he started off
  That morning, leaving the town to the others,
  Entering the high-woods tipped in pink

By the rising sun but still dark where he walked.
"This is the way," he continued as he watched
  For the great space that he felt sure

Would open before him, a stark sea over which
  The turbulent sky would drop the shadowy shapes
  Of its song, and he would move his arms

And begin to mark, almost as a painter would,
  The passages of greater and lesser worth, the silken
  Tropes and calls to this or that, coarsely conceived,

Echoing and blasting all around. He would whip them
  Into shape. Everything would have an edge. The burning
  Will of weather, blowing overhead, would be his muse.

"This is the life," he said, as he reached the first
  Of many outer edges to the sea he sought, and he buttoned
  His coat, and turned up his collar, and began to breathe.

Dark Harbor

I

In the night without end, in the soaking dark,
I am wearing a white suit that shines
Among the black leaves falling, among

The insect-covered moons of the street lamps.
I am walking among the emerald trees
In the night without end. I am crossing

The street and disappearing around the corner.
I shine as I go through the park on my way
To the station where the others are waiting.

Soon we shall travel through the soundless dark,
With fires guiding us over the bitter terrain
Of the night without end. I am wearing

A suit that outdoes the moon, that is pure sheen
As I come to the station where the others
Are whispering, saying that the moon

Is no more a hindrance than anything else,
That, if anyone suffers, wings can be had
For a song or by trading arms, that the rules

On earth still hold for those about to depart,
That it is best to be ready, for the ash
Of the body is worthless and goes only so far.

I I

I am writing from a place you have never been,
Where the trains don't run, and planes
Don't land, a place to the west,

Where heavy hedges of snow surround each house,
Where the wind screams at the moon's blank face,
Where the people are plain, and fashions,

If they come, come late and are seen
As forms of oppression, sources of sorrow.
This is a place that sparkles a bit at 7 p.m.,

Then goes out, and slides into the funeral home
Of the stars, and everyone dreams of floating
Like angels in sweet-smelling habits,

Of being released from sundry services
Into the round of pleasures there for the asking—
Days like pages torn from a family album,

Endless reunions, the heavenly choir at the barbecue
Adjusting its tone to serve the occasion,
And everyone staring, stunned into magnitude.

III

Go in any direction and you will return to the main drag.
Something about the dull little shops, the useless items
That turn into necessities, a sense of direction,

Even the feel of becoming yourself on your return,
As you pass through the outskirts, the rows of houses
Aglow with an icy green from TVs, spreading

A sheen of familiarity, of deliverance, as you
Make your way back to the center where, because of the hour
The streets are deserted except for the slow passage of cars,

And here and there somebody standing for no reason,
Holding a letter in her hand or holding a leash
With no dog at the end, casting a shadow,

And you pass by unsure if this coming back is a failure
Or a sign of success, a sign that the time has come
To embrace your origins as you would yourself,

That staying away no longer makes sense, even if no one
Is shedding tears over the folly or wisdom of your decision;
The world has always gotten along without you,

Which is why you left home in the first place,
So what about those shops and the empty luminous cones
Of light that fall from the lamps, and the echo of your own steps?

From far away, life looked to be simpler back in the town
You started from . . . look, there in the kitchen are Mom and Dad,
He's reading the paper, she's killing a fly.

I V

There is a certain triviality in living here,
A lightness, a comic monotony that one tries
To undermine with shows of energy, a devotion

To the vagaries of desire, whereas over there
Is a seriousness, a stiff, inflexible gloom
That shrouds the disappearing soul, a weight

That shames our lightness. Just look
Across the river and you will discover
How unworthy you are as you describe what you see,

Which is bound by what is available.
On the other side, no one is looking this way.
They are committed to obstacles,

To the textures and levels of darkness,
To the tedious enactment of duration.
And they labor not for bread or love

But to perpetuate the balance between the past
And the future. They are the future as it
Extends itself, just as we are the past

Coming to terms with itself. Which is why
The napkins are pressed, and the cookies have come
On time, and why the glass of milk, looking so chic

In its whiteness, begs us to sip. None of this happens
Over there. Relief from anything is seen
As timid, a sign of shallowness or worse.

V

The soldiers are gone, and now the women are leaving.
The dogs howl at the moon, and the moon flees
Through the clouds. I wonder if I shall ever catch up.

I think of the shining cheeks, the serious palettes
Of my friends, and I am sure I am not of their company.
There was a time when I was touched by the pallor of truth,

When the fatal steps I took seemed more like the drift
Of summer crossed at times by the scented music of rain,
But that was before I was waved to the side

By the officer on duty, and told that henceforth
I would have to invent my pleasure, carve it out of the air,
Subtract it from my future. And I could have no illusions;

A mysterious crape would cover my work. The roll of a drum
Would govern the fall of my feet in the long corridors.
"And listen," the officer said, "on any morning look down

Into the valley. Watch the shadows, the clouds dispersing
Then look through the ice into nature's frozen museum,
See how perfectly everything fits in its space."

VI

Where would it end and how would it matter
If the world, illumined by the dawning moon,
Were to break in on everyone's sleep,

And desire that is everywhere in dreams were released
And reached not for the whole earth which everyone
Thinks is its likely object, but instead grew

Into an enlarged desire, a desire that wished for even more,
For an unthinkable conclusion, an impossible satisfaction,
Itself increasing, enclosing within its appetite

The elaboration and extension of its despair,
The dark underside of growth that says to the pleasure
Of wishing there will be no satisfaction adequate,

That even on these silver lawns and sidewalks,
For which the midnight air of late October seems
The only possible accompaniment, no sign

Of satisfaction is possible. There is only
Larger and larger dissatisfaction. Only teeth
Tearing and gnawing. Everything always larger and more

Elusive, with the weight of the future saying
That I am only what you are, but more so.
And you, without allowing yourself time

For exhaustion, pursue this promise because
It is yours, the loss that is continuous
Will be all yours and will only increase.

VII

O you can make fun of the splendors of moonlight,
But what would the human heart be if it wanted
Only the dark, wanted nothing on earth

But the sea's ink or the rock's black shade?
On a summer night to launch yourself into the silver
Emptiness of air and look over the pale fields

At rest under the sullen stare of the moon,
And to linger in the depths of your vision and wonder
How in this whiteness what you love is past

Grief, and how in the long valley of your looking
Hope grows, and there, under the distant,
Barely perceptible fire of all the stars,

To feel yourself wake into change, as if your change
Were immense and figured into the heavens' longing.
And yet all you want is to rise out of the shade

Of yourself into the cooling blaze of a summer night
When the moon shines and the earth itself
Is covered and silent in the stoniness of its sleep.

VIII

If dawn breaks the heart, and the moon is a horror,
And the sun is nothing but the source of torpor,
Then of course I would have been silent all these years

And would not have chosen to go out tonight
In my new dark blue double-breasted suit
And to sit in a restaurant with a bowl

Of soup before me to celebrate how good life
Has been and how it has culminated in this instant.
The harmonies of wholesomeness have reached their apogee,

And I am aquiver with satisfaction, and you look
Good, too. I love your gold teeth and your dyed hair—
A little green, a little yellow—and your weight,

Which is finally up where we never thought
It would be. O my partner, my beautiful death,
My black paradise, my fusty intoxicant,

My symbolist muse, give me your breast
Or your hand or your tongue that sleeps all day
Behind its wall of reddish gums.

Lay yourself down on the restaurant floor
And recite all that's been kept from my happiness.
Tell me I have not lived in vain, that the stars

Will not die, that things will stay as they are,
That what I have seen will last, that I was not born
Into change, that what I have said has not been said for me.

I X

Where is the experience that meant so much,
That carried such weight? Where is it now
If not lodged in memory, in the air of memory,

In the place that is not a place, but where
The mortal beauty of the world is stored.
Oh yes, we are busy under the moon's gaze,

Its mouth giving back a silent O of surprise
Each time we try to explain how it was,
How fleeting, breakable, expensive it was.

We are always about to take off into a future
Unencumbered, as if we could leave ourselves behind,
But of course we never do. Who can face the future,

Especially now, as a nobody with no past
To fall back on, nothing to prove one is
Like everyone else, with baby pictures

And pictures of Mom and Dad in their old-fashioned
Swimsuits on a beach somewhere in the Maritimes.
We are at work on the past to make the future

More bearable. Ah, the potential past, how it swells,
How it crowds the days before us with feelings
And postures we had dismissed until now.

X

It is a dreadful cry that rises up,
Hoping to be heard, that comes to you
As you wake, so your day will be spent

In the futile correction of a distant longing.
All those voices calling from the depths of elsewhere,
From the abyss of an August night, from the misery

Of a northern winter, from a ship going down in the Baltic,
From heartache, from wherever you wish, calling to be saved.
And you have no choice but to follow their prompting,

Saving something of that sound, urging the harsh syllables
Of disaster into music. You stare out the window,
Watching the build-up of clouds, and the wind whipping

The branches of a willow, sending a rain of leaves
To the ground. How do you turn pain
Into its own memorial, how do you write it down,

Turning it into itself as witnessed
Through pleasure, so it can be known, even loved,
As it lives in what it could not be.

XI

A long time has passed and yet it seems
Like yesterday, in the midmost moment of summer,
When we felt the disappearance of sorrow,

And saw beyond the rough stone walls
The flesh of clouds, heavy with the scent
Of the southern desert, rise in a prodigal

Overflowing of mildness. It seems like yesterday
When we stood by the iron gate in the center
Of town while the pollen-filled breath

Of the wind drew the shadow of the clouds
Around us so that we could feel the force
Of our freedom while still the captives of dark.

And later when the rain fell and flooded the streets
And we heard the dripping on the porch and the wind
Rustling the leaves like paper, how to explain

Our happiness then, the particular way our voices
Erased all signs of the sorrow that had been,
Its violence, its terrible omens of the end?

XII

So it came of its own like the sun that covers
The damp grass with its luster and drives the cold
Into the dark corners of the house; out of silence

It came, and, as we were not exactly wild
With anticipation, it waited awhile at the verge
Of recognition, growing in importance

And urgency but still without a message
To deliver, until the wind blew just so
And formed a formidable catspaw

On the water, at which point for some reason,
We knew it had come at last—the sense that we were
To make of such an appearance, its sudden arrival,

How it crowded out everything else. And now
The panorama of the lake was charged
With the arrival of a cloud whose purpose

We would have to decipher and apply
To our own ends, so we could say that it came
For further clarification, some heavy editing,

As it pitched itself forward, casting a shade,
A vague sense, over the lake and us,
Which would end in either dismissal or doubt.

XIII

The mist clears. The morning mountains
Range themselves beyond the placid town.
The light-footed deer come down to the graveyard,

And the magpies cry. All is well.
It is the moment to resist the onset
Of another average day, to beat the daylight

For exotic instances of this or that.
We must let out the pigs, pink and snorting,
To wander the neighborhood, we must

Let out the cows as well, and let them
Lounge on the lawns of the major houses.
There's lots to be done. For instance,

Make imprecision the core of the school
Curriculum so that years from now we will appear
Unchanged, make sadness another required course,

So that it can be known without
Personal involvement. There is little time left.
None for a drink at the local bistro,

None for a pointless stroll, none for a change
Of clothes. We must get down to work: mail the pajamas
To Esther in Holland, paint the sidewalk,

Move the dying piano out to the beach.
If only it were possible to spruce up the air
Without buying a spruce, the day might begin

To take on a light of its own, green and piercing.

XIV

The ship has been held in the harbor.
The promise of departure has begun to dim.
The radiance of the sea, the shining abundance

Of its blue are nevertheless undiminished.
The will of the passengers struggles to release
The creaking ship. All they want

Is one last voyage beyond the papery palms
And the shoals of melancholy, beyond the glass
And alabaster mansions strung along

The shores, beyond the siren sounds
And the grinding gears of big trucks climbing the hills,
Out into the moonlit bareness of waves,

Where watery scrawls tempt the voyager to reach down
And hold the dissolving messages in his palm.
Again and again the writing surfaces,

Shines a moment in the light, then sinks unread.
Why should the passengers want so badly
To glimpse what they shall never have?

Why are so many of them crowded at the rail,
With the ship still dozing in the harbor?
And to whom are they waving? It has been

Years since the stores in town were open,
Years since the flag was raised in the little park,
Since the cloud behind the nearby mountain moved.

X V

What light is this that says the air is golden,
That even the green trees can be saved
For a moment and look bejeweled,

That my hand, as I lift it over the shade
Of my body, becomes a flame pointing the way
To a world from which no one returns, yet towards

Which everyone travels? The sheen of the possible
Is adjusting itself to a change of venue: the look
Of farewell, the sun dipping under the clouds,

Faltering at the serrated edge of the mountains,
Then going quickly. And the new place, the night,
Spacious, empty, a tomb of lights, turning away,

And going under, becoming what no one remembers.

XVI

It is true, as someone has said, that in
A world without heaven all is farewell.
Whether you wave your hand or not,

It is farewell, and if no tears come to your eyes
It is still farewell, and if you pretend not to notice,
Hating what passes, it is still farewell.

Farewell no matter what. And the palms as they lean
Over the green, bright lagoon, and the pelicans
Diving, and the glistening bodies of bathers resting,

Are stages in an ultimate stillness, and the movement
Of sand, and of wind, and the secret moves of the body
Are part of the same, a simplicity that turns being

Into an occasion for mourning, or into an occasion
Worth celebrating, for what else does one do,
Feeling the weight of the pelicans' wings,

The density of the palms' shadows, the cells that darken
The backs of bathers? These are beyond the distortions
Of chance, beyond the evasions of music. The end

Is enacted again and again. And we feel it
In the temptations of sleep, in the moon's ripening,
In the wine as it waits in the glass.

XVII

I have just said goodbye to a friend
And am staring at fields of cornstalks.
Their stubble is being burned, and the smoke

Forms a gauze over the sun's blank face.
Off to the side there is a line of poplars.
And beyond, someone is driving a tractor.

Does he live in that little white house?
Someone is playing a tape of birds singing.
Someone has fallen asleep on a boxcar of turnips.

I think of the seasonal possibilities.
O pretty densities of white on white!
O snowflake lost in the vestibules of April air!

Beyond the sadness—the empty restaurants,
The empty streets, the small lamps shining
Down on the town—I see only the stretches

Of ice and snow, the straight pines, the frigid moon.

XVIII

"I would like to step out of my heart's door and be
Under the great sky." I would like to step out
And be on the other side, and be part of all

That surrounds me. I would like to be
In that solitude of soundless things, in the random
Company of the wind, to be weightless, nameless.

But not for long, for I would be downcast without
The things I keep inside my heart; and in no time
I would be back. Ah! the old heart

In which I sleep, in which my sleep increases, in which
My grief is ponderous, in which the leaves are falling,
In which the streets are long, in which the night

Is dark, in which the sky is great, the old heart
That murmurs to me of what cannot go on,
Of the dancing, of the inmost dancing.

XIX

I go out and sit on my roof, hoping
That a creature from another planet will see me
And say, "There's life on earth, definitely life;

"See that earthling on top of his home,
His manifold possessions under him,
Let's name him after our planet." Whoa!

X X

Is it you standing among the olive trees
Beyond the courtyard? You in the sunlight
Waving me closer with one hand while the other

Shields your eyes from the brightness that turns
All that is not you dead white? Is it you
Around whom the leaves scatter like foam?

You in the murmuring night that is scented
With mint and lit by the distant wilderness
Of stars? Is it you? Is it really you

Rising from the script of waves, the length
Of your body casting a sudden shadow over my hand
So that I feel how cold it is as it moves

Over the page? You leaning down and putting
Your mouth against mine so I should know
That a kiss is only the beginning

Of what until now we could only imagine?
Is it you or the long compassionate wind
That whispers in my ear: alas, alas?

XXI

Low shadows skim the earth, a few clouds bleed,
A couple of grazing cows carry the next world
On their backs, their hides the mysterious maps

Of the principal countries. Too bad the future
Is covered with flies, and sits in a pasture.
Here comes old age, dragging a tale of soft

Inconvenience, of golfing in Florida,
Of gumming bad food. These cows never stop chewing.
O love, how did we get here, so far from the coast

Of our friends, our nervous talkative friends
Who are now reading in bed or watching TV
Because it is later there, and they must

Keep their minds off missing us, off whatever
Would happen were we to come back from our exile?
And the earth is almost dark, the crickets

Are clicking, the laundry is in the dryer,
The heat of the night is giving us new things
To wish for. Who cares if we were young once—

The young don't care, the old don't care,
So long as they are not left behind.

XXII

It happened years ago and in somebody else's
Dining room. Madame X begged to be relieved
Of a sexual pain that had my name

Written all over it. Those were the days
When so many things of a sexual nature seemed to happen,
And my name—I believed—was written on all of them.

Madame X took my hand under the table, placed it
On her thigh, then moved it up. You would never know
What a woman with such blue eyes and blond hair

Was not wearing. Did I suffer,
Knowing that I was wanted for the wrong reasons?
Of course, and it has taken me years to recover.

We don't give parties like that anymore.
These days we sit around and sigh.
We like the sound of it, and it seems to combine

Weariness and judgment, even to suggest
No eggs for the moment, no sausages either,
Just come, take me away, and put me to bed.

XXIII

And suddenly we heard the explosion.
A man who'd been cramped and bloated for weeks
Blew wide open. His wife, whose back was to him,

Didn't turn right away to give everything—
The cheese and soggy bread—a chance to settle.
She was a beauty, and considered a cunning cook,

But there were things she did not share with the rest of us.
So the fact that her back was turned was important.
We seemed to sense that she and her husband

Hadn't been seeing eye to eye. But that was as far as we got
Even though we questioned her culinary skills and what
Had driven her to blow up her husband, and we wondered—

Each of the men in the room—if she considered
Blowing us up. It happened that she left town
Before we could ask. No charges were pressed

So she sold the house and moved
To a large southern city where no one would know
The dangers of being invited to her house for dinner.

XXIV

Now think of the weather and how it is rarely the same
For any two people, how when it is small, precision is needed
To say when it is really an aura or odor or even an air

Of certainty, or how, as the hours go by, it could be thought of
As large because of the number of people it touches.
Its strength is something else: tornados are small

But strong and cloudless summer days seem infinite
But tend to be weak since we don't mind being out in them.
Excuse me, is this the story of another exciting day,

The sort of thing that accompanies preparations for dinner?
Then what say we talk about the inaudible—the shape it assumes,
And what social implications it holds,

Or the somber flourishes of autumn—the bright
Or blighted leaves falling, the clicking of cold branches,
The new color of the sky, its random blue.

XXV

Is what exists a souvenir of the time
Of the great nought and deep night without stars.
The time before the universe began?

When we look at each other and see nothing
Is that not a confirmation that we are less
Than meets the eye and embody some of

The night of our origins, and isn't everything
A little less than meets the eye, reminding us
That our ignorance is verified by the nothing

Which it honors? And isn't it true that
A loss of memory is the most powerful force
In the formation of culture, that the past

Is always simplified to make room for
The present? And aren't we more interested
In what may happen or will happen

Than in what has already happened, and so look ahead
Into the dark and imagine a fullness in which
We are the stars, matching the emptiness

Of the beginning, giving birth to ourselves
Again and again, rising out of the ruins or ashes
Of the past? Our images blaze a path

That our poor bodies must follow. And the wind
That pursues is the perfumed wind of spring
That promises much, but settles for summer.

XXVI

I have come from my cabin, from my place high
In the Rockies, have trod down narrow gravel trails,
Slogged through bogs and mud flats, have come

Into the broad valley and, without food
And drink, crossed it, and all the while
Murmured your name to myself, and as I did

I was filled with a shuddering, something
Like ecstasy, and was on the verge of losing
My way, but never did; I just kept coming;

Nothing could hold me back, not the sudden
Soaking downpours, not the stretches of clogging heat,
Nothing. I staggered forward, unshaven, limping,

My clothes ragged, I came in my vileness, believing
That you, understanding my passion, would forgive me,
And after the reading, O my master, that you would

Open the copy of your book, which I brought with me,
Taped to my back so that it wouldn't get
Dirty or stolen, and sign it and say a kind word

Or offer best wishes to me, one of the many
Worshippers of your work and himself a practitioner,
So that on the worst days it will be possible

For me to open it and feel wanted, and to know,
In my lingering over your signature, Master, the power
Of your wisdom as you have passed it on to me.

XXVII

Of this one I love how the beautiful echoed
Within the languorous length of his sentences,
Forming a pleasing pointless commotion;

Of another the figures pushing each other
Out of the way, the elaborate overcharged
Thought threatening always to fly apart;

Of another the high deliberate tone,
The diction tending towards falseness
But always falling perfectly short;

Of another the rush and vigor of observation,
The speed of disclosure, the aroused intelligence
Exerting itself, lifting the poem into prophecy;

Of this one the humor, the struggle to locate high art
Anywhere but expected, and to gild the mundane
With the force of the demonic or the angelic;

Of yet another the precision, the pursuit of rightness,
Balance, some ineffable decorum, the measured, circuitous
Stalking of the subject, turning surprise to revelation;

And that leaves this one on the side of his mountain,
Hunched over the page, thanking his loves for coming
And keeping him company all this time.

XXVIII

There is a luminousness, a convergence of enchantments,
And the world is altered for the better as trees,
Rivers, mountains, animals, all find their true place,

But only while Orpheus sings. When the song is over
The world resumes its old flaws, and things are again
Mismatched and misplaced and the cruelty of men

Is tempered only by laws. Orpheus can change the world
For a while, but he cannot save it, which is his despair.
It is a brilliant limitation he enacts and

He knows it, which is why the current of his song
Is always mournful, always sad. It is even worse
For the rest of us. As someone has said, ". . . we barely begin

And paralysis takes over, forcing us out for a breath
Of fresh air." As if that wasn't bad enough, he says,
"But though reams of work do get done, not much listens.

I have the feeling my voice is just for me . . ." There is
A current of resignation that charges even our most
Determined productions. Still, we feel better for trying,

And there is always a glass of wine to restore us
To our former majesty, to the well of our wishes
In which we are mirrored, but darkly as though

A shadowed glass held within its frozen calm an image
Of abundance, a bloom of humanness, a hymn in which
The shapes and sounds of Paradise are buried.

XXIX

The folded memory of our great and singular elevations,
The tragic slapping of vowels to produce tears,
The heavy golden grieving in our dreams,

Shaping the soul's solemn sounds on the edge of speech
That carry the fullness of intention and the emptiness
Of achievement are not quite the savage

Knowledge of ourselves that refuses to correct itself
But lumbers instead into formless affirmation,
Saying selfhood is hating Dad or wanting Mom,

Is being kissed by a reader somewhere, is about me
And all my minutes circulating around me like flies—
Me at my foulest, the song of me, me in the haunted

Woods of my own condition, a solitaire but never alone.
These are bad times. Idiots have stolen the moonlight.
They cast their shadowy pomp wherever they wish.

XXX

There is a road through the canyon,
A river beside the road, a forest.
If there is more, I haven't seen it yet.

Still, it is possible to say this has been
An amazing century for fashion if for nothing else;
The way brave models held back their tears

When thinking of the millions of Jews and Serbs
That Hitler killed, and how the photographer
Steadied his hand when he considered

The Muzhiks that Stalin took care of.
The way skirts went up and down; how breasts
Were in, then out; and the long and the short of hair.

But the road that winds through the canyon
Is covered with snow, and the river flows
Under the ice. Cross-country skiers are moving

Like secrets between the trees of the glassed-in forest.
The day has made a fabulous cage of cold around
My face. Whenever I take a breath I hear cracking.

XXXI

Here we are in Labrador. I've always
Wanted to be here, especially with you,
In this cabin, with a fire blazing. You are

Wearing a Calvin Klein suit and I am in
My father's velvet smoking jacket. That's all.
Why? Because I am happy. And I am ready

For the first sign from you that we should
Get into bed. These moments of giddy anticipation
Are the happiest of my life. I wonder if we

Are not part of someone's prediction of what
The world could be at its very best, if we,
In this frigid landscape free of shopping

Opportunities, are where the world is headed?
Or maybe we are part of the record of what
Has already happened, and are a sign of the depths

To which the world sank? Your costly suit,
My shabby jacket, this cabin without indoor
Plumbing or decent stove or stereo or TV

May be no more than a joke in the final
Tally of accomplishments to be claimed
At some late date. Still, here we are

And they can't take that away from us,
And if they laugh, so what, we're here,
Happy in Labrador, dancing into the wee hours.

XXXII

Out here, dwarfed by mountains and a sky of fires
And round rocks, in the academy of revelations
Which gets smaller every year, we have come

To see ourselves as less and do not like
Shows of abundance, descriptions we cannot believe,
When a simple still life—roses in an azure bowl—does fine.

The idea of our being large is inconceivable,
Even after lunch with Harry at Lutece, even after
Finishing *The Death of Virgil*. The image of a god,

A platonic person, who does not breathe or bleed,
But brings whole rooms, whole continents to light,
Like the sun, is not for us. We have a growing appetite

For littleness, a piece of ourselves, a bit of the world,
An understanding that remains unfinished, unentire,
Largely imperfect so long as it lasts.

XXXIII

I was visiting the shabby villa of a friend,
Full of rooms curtained against the sun,
With marble floors uncarpeted and cold.

He had invited a few Russian women
For dinner. I remember liking the custard,
Which none of the other guests touched.

I felt alone. The women began to blow
Out the candles. I wondered if they, too, had been
To the Delicatessen of Love. No, they had been

To Italy, they said. When I returned to my room,
I put on my overcoat and got into bed.
Soon I heard a rustling outside my door.

"It's me, Olga, may I come in?" When she came in,
I got out of bed, took off my clothes, and stood
in front of the mirror. She joined me. "Finally,

We are safe from one another," she said. "Yes,"
I admitted somewhat sadly, "in the mirror the body
Becomes simultaneously visible and untouchable."

And so, in the gloomy villa we spent the night
Staring at our naked bodies, cold, shining,
While a fair fire roared in the hearth.

XXXIV

It's a pity that nature no longer means
The woods, nor the wilds, nor even our own
Worst behavior, nor the behavior of

Certain creatures. It's a pity we cannot
Believe that man and nature are essentially
Adapted to each other, that "the mind of man"

Mirrors "the fairest and most interesting
Qualities of nature." Now that nature includes
Oblivion, in which we dare not see ourselves,

We stand under the hollow moon and hear
No praising harp strings or mournful talk
To move us closer to the unreachables—

The silences and distances in which we walk
And feel ourselves available to all
That bends us towards each other.

The wind is hollow. The world is strange,
Part of an order, larger than and oblivious
To the life that gathers upon it.

X X X V

The sickness of angels is nothing new.
I have seen them crawling like bees,
Flightless, chewing their tongues, not singing,

Down by the bus terminal, hanging out,
Showing their legs, hiding their wings,
Carrying on for their brief term on earth,

No longer smiling; asleep in the shade of each other
They drift into the arms of strangers who step
Into their light, which is the mascara of Eden,

Offering more than invisible love,
Intangible comforts, offering the taste,
The pure erotic glory of death without echoes,

The feel of kisses blown out of heaven,
Melting the moment they land.

XXXVI

I cannot decide whether or not to stroll
Through the somber garden where the grass in the shade
Is silver and frozen and where the general green

Of the rest of the garden is dark except
For a luminous patch made by the light of a window.
I cannot decide, and because it is autumn

When the sadness of gardens is greatest, I believe
That someone is already there and is waiting
For the pale appearance of another. She sits

On one of the benches, breathing the sweet
Rotten odors of leaves trapped under the trees, and feels
The sudden cold, a seasonal chill, the distant breath

Of coming rain. So many silent battles are waged
By those who sit alone and wait, and by those who delay.
By the time I arrive the snow has whitened my hair,

And placed on my shoulders two glittering, tiny
Epaulettes. I could be a major in Napoleon's army,
Which might be the reason she asks me:

Why would someone invade a poor country
Like this, a garden near the end of its life
With a woman inside it, unless he was lonely

And would do what he must to stave off the long
Campaigns of unhappiness that level everything,
Making rebuilding impossible, especially in winter?

XXXVII

On Sunday she sits in a silver chair in an echoing hall,
Wearing the cold clothes of a widow, as if she were one,
Hearing the cries of the wind among the twisted trees.

If there were someone there, she would speak
Of what it is like to wait without hope, to watch
The daylight inch across the floor,

Or maybe she would say that death is easier if everywhere
One looks is Hell, and there is nowhere else to go.
Orpheus came to visit her, came several times.

Each time he left he wished her well, but he was a fool,
Preferring the moonlit chords of his melancholy,
The inward drift of notes to anything of hers. And yet,

What does it matter now? He's gone for good. The floating
Darkness of the cries seems more and more the prompting
Of a distant will, a fatal music rising everywhere.

XXXVIII

And so he appears at the back of the hall.
The rest is up to me. To say, for example,
Why he has come and where he has come from,

And why for this occasion he has chosen to wear
A hat when nobody these days wears a hat,
And why he wears it pulled down so the brim

Just clears his eyes. He never smiles,
He never shifts his weight. He merely stands
And stares as if in the severity

Of his motionlessness he were a stand-in
For somebody or something, an idea
Of withdrawal or silence, for instance,

Or for the perfection of watchfulness, how
It entraps by casting an invisible net
Around the watched, paralyzing him,

Turning him into a watcher as well,
A watcher who sees and must say what he sees,
Must carve a figure out of blankness,

Invent it in other words so that it has meaning,
Which is the burden of invention, its
Awkward weight, which must fit the man's

Appearance, the way he raises a hand
And extends it at arm's length, holding within it
A small gun, which he points at the one who assumed

The responsibility of watching, and now he squeezes
The trigger and the gun goes off and something falls,
A fragment, a piece of a larger intention, that is all.

XXXIX

When after a long silence one picks up the pen
And leans over the paper and says to himself:
Today I shall consider Marsyas

Whose body was flayed to excess,
Who made no crime that would square
With what he was made to suffer.

Today I shall consider the shredded remains of Marsyas—
What do they mean as they gather the sunlight
That falls in pieces through the trees,

As in Titian's late painting? Poor Marsyas,
A body, a body of work as it turns and falls
Into suffering, becoming the flesh of light,

Which is fed to onlookers centuries later.
Can this be the cost of encompassing pain?
After a long silence, would I, whose body

Is whole, sheltered, kept in the dark by a mind
That prefers it that way, know what I'd done
And what its worth was? Or is a body scraped

From the bone of experience, the chart of suffering
To be read in such ways that all flesh might be redeemed,
At least for the moment, the moment it passes into song.

X L

How can I sing when I haven't the heart, or the hope
That something of paradise persists in my song,
That a touch of those long afternoons of summer

Flowing with golden greens under the sky's unbroken blue
Will find a home in yet another imagined place?
Will someone be there to play the viola, someone for whom

The sad tunes still matter? And after I go, as I must,
And come back through the hourglass, will I have proved
That I live against time, that the silk of the songs

I sang is not lost? Or will I have proved that whatever I love
Is unbearable, that the views of Lethe will never
Improve, that whatever I sing is a blank?

XLI

Sometimes after dinner when I wander out,
And stare into the night sky and realize I have no idea
Of what I see, that the distance of the stars

Is meaningless and their number far beyond
What I can reckon, I wonder if the physicist
Sees the same sky I do, a lavish ordering of lights,

Disposed to match our scale, and our power to imagine
In simple terms a space like the space we suffer
Here on earth in this room with you sitting

In that chair, reading a book of which I understand
Nothing, thinking thoughts I could not guess at,
As moments approach whose cargo is a mystery.

Ah, who knows! We are already travelling faster than our
Apparent stillness can stand, and if it keeps up
You will be light-years away by the time I speak.

XLII

Our friends who lumbered from room to room
Now move like songs or meditations winding down,
Or lie about, waiting for the next good thing—

Some news of what is going on above,
A visitor to tell them who's writing well,
Who's falling in or out of love.

Not that it matters anymore. Just look around.
There's Marsyas, noted for his marvelous asides
On Athena's ancient oboe, asleep for centuries.

And Arion, whose gaudy music drove the Phrygians wild,
Hasn't spoken in a hundred years. The truth is
Soon the song deserts its maker,

The airy demon dies, and others come along.
A different kind of dark invades the autumn woods,
A different sound sends lovers packing into sleep.

The air is full of anguish. The measures of nothingness
Are few. The Beyond is merely beyond,
A melancholy place of failed and fallen stars.

XLIII

All afternoon I have thought how alike
Are "The Lament of the Pianos Heard in Rich Neighborhoods"
And "Piano Practice at the Academy of the Holy Angels,"

And how the girls that played are no longer here. Yet it was never
A vast music that mingled with the lusters of the room,
Nothing that would drown our desire for rest or silence.

It was just there like the source of delight—
Unblemished, unobserved—though things did not always turn out
    well.
As now the green leaves brood under an early snow,

And the houses are darkened by time. The sounds of summer
Have left. The purple woods, which color the distance,
Form a farewell for the monotonous autumn.

The snows have come, and the black shapes of the pianos
Are sleeping and cannot be roused, like the girls themselves
Who have gone, and the leaves, and all that was just here.

XLIV

I recall that I stood before the breaking waves,
Afraid not of the water so much as the noise,
That I covered my ears and ran to my mother

And waited to be taken away to the house in town
Where it was quiet, with no sound of the sea anywhere near.
Yet the sea itself, the sight of it, the way it spread

As far as we could see, was thrilling.
Only its roar was frightening. And now years later
It is the sound as well as its size that I love

And miss in my inland exile among the mountains
That do not change except for the light
That colors them or the snows that make them remote

Or the clouds that lift them, so they appear much higher
Than they are. They are acted upon and have none
Of the mystery of the sea that generates its own changes.

Encounters with each are bound to differ,
Yet if I had to choose I would look at the sea
And lose myself in its sounds which so frightened me once.

But in those days what did I know of the pleasures of loss,
Of the edge of the abyss coming close with its hisses
And storms, a great watery animal breaking itself on the rocks,

Sending up stars of salt, loud clouds of spume.

X L V

I am sure you would find it misty here,
With lots of stone cottages badly needing repair.
Groups of souls, wrapped in cloaks, sit in the fields

Or stroll the winding unpaved roads. They are polite,
And oblivious to their bodies, which the wind passes through,
Making a shushing sound. Not long ago,

I stopped to rest in a place where an especially
Thick mist swirled up from the river. Someone,
Who claimed to have known me years before,

Approached, saying there were many poets
Wandering around who wished to be alive again.
They were ready to say the words they had been unable to say—

Words whose absence had been the silence of love,
Of pain, and even of pleasure. Then he joined a small group,
Gathered beside a fire. I believe I recognized

Some of the faces, but as I approached they tucked
Their heads under their wings. I looked away to the hills
Above the river, where the golden lights of sunset

And sunrise are one and the same, and saw something flying
Back and forth, fluttering its wings. Then it stopped in mid-air.
It was an angel, one of the good ones, about to sing.

NOTES

A Note About the Author

Mark Strand is the winner of the Pulitzer Prize in poetry and a former Poet Laureate. He has written nine books of poems, which have brought him many honors and grants, including a MacArthur Fellowship. He is the author of a book of stories, *Mr. and Mrs. Baby*, several volumes of translations (of works by Raphael Alberti and Carlos Drummond de Andrade, among others), the editor of a number of anthologies, and author of several monographs on contemporary artists (William Bailey and Edward Hopper). He was born in Summerside, Prince Edward Island, Canada, and was raised and educated in the United States. He teaches currently at the Committee on Social Thought at the University of Chicago.

A Note on the Type

This book was set on the Linotype in Janson, a recutting made direct from type cast from matrices long thought to have been made by the Dutchman Anton Janson, who was a practicing type founder in Leipzig during the years 1668–1687. However, it has been conclusively demonstrated that these types are actually the work of Nicholas Kis (1650–1702), a Hungarian, who most probably learned his trade from the master Dutch type founder Dirk Voskens. The type is an excellent example of the influential and sturdy Dutch types that prevailed in England up to the time William Caslon developed his own incomparable designs from them.

Composition by Heritage Printers, Inc.,
Charlotte, North Carolina
Designed by Harry Ford

Printed in the United States
by Baker & Taylor Publisher Services